Cute as a

Button,

TOUGH AS A GIRL

A Memoir

Cute as a Button,

TOUGH AS A GIRL

A Memoir

CHERINA JOHNSON

Dedication

In loving memory of my parents -

Mary Loyd Deal, my biggest and loudest fan and
most fierce protector. Also, the one who passed
on to me her beautiful looks

Carl C. Frazier, the one who passed on to me the athletic
gene and shared with me the love for the game

Contents

Introduction

*O*nce upon a time, there was a young girl whose life was set on a course never imagined by way of a fateful announcement made on the school intercom system. It was the end of the 4th grade school year when an announcement was made on the intercom for next year's girls' 5th and 6th grade basketball team tryout. For some reason, I had a desire to attend. This was strange because I had no prior basketball experience. On top of that, I could not recall that I had even dribbled a basketball a day in my life. Nevertheless, it was as though I was being drawn in like a magnet. I made up my mind that I would go to the tryout. This would later prove to be a very pivotal decision that would set me on a fateful course in my life.

When I attended the tryout, the coaches taught us a series of basketball drills. To my surprise, I was able to dribble the ball. Not only that but I could also hit the rim shooting from the free throw line. This was a major revelation being that I had not played basketball before. After the tryout, yours truly made the cut to play on the team the following year.

During my inaugural basketball year, there were a few instances that proved to be very instrumental in my life, a lot of life lessons. First, my coaches were two female teachers from the same school who were both coaching for the first time. This was just as much a learning experience for them as it was for me and safe to say for the rest of my teammates as well. We all grew and learned the game of basketball together. Second, parents and other adults took elementary basketball games very seriously. My mom was definitely one of the ring leaders in this area. From the beginning of my basketball career, she was my biggest and loudest supporter, as well as my fierce protector. Momma Bear took it seriously and personally when it came to her cub. I will elaborate on this in more detail later. Third, you will find out what is inside you when you are challenged and called out by your coaches and others. Fourth, winning is a team effort for a common goal, each one playing their part to bring the goal to pass. Fifth, playing an organized sport helps to develop and mature lifelong skills and long-term relationships.

Growing up people would often comment that I was pretty. This was passed down to me from my Creator through my very beautiful mother. This proved to be such an asset to me throughout my basketball career. People often underestimated me based on my looks. Many assumed that I could not play ball or did not initially take me seriously as a player, especially the boys. Once I recognized that at a young age, I used it to my advantage. Despite my outward appearance, there was another part of me that went unseen by the natural eye. I was a competitor and hated to lose. The inward part was more important than my outward features which would repeatedly prove you should not judge a book by its cover.

Throughout my basketball years, it was natural and very important to me to exhibit my feminine nature. This was critical in my childhood years because it showed me that a person could be cute, as well as tough at the same time. The title of this book was birthed from this fact. It is a pet peeve of mine for girls or women to try to look and act masculine in order to appear tough. Do not get me wrong, everyone is entitled to do what they want to do regarding this. But ask yourself, is it to express yourself or to portray an image? Who said you had to look like or act like a boy to be able to compete with the boys? Embracing and displaying my femininity in the competitive sport of basketball was very powerful! I used it to my advantage and brought down a lot of male egos in the process.

LIFE LESSONS:

- Looks can be deceiving. Remember the adage, "Don't judge a book by its cover."
- Femininity does not equal weakness
- You will get out what you put in

Actions Speak Louder Than Words

Typically, I was not a talker on the court. I was not one of those people who would run off their mouths and talk all kind of junk to others on the court. These were the people that I would purpose to shut up. My preference was to let my actions speak for me. Outwardly I was quiet, but rest assured I was fired up on the inside. It was time to go to work and hopefully send someone off the court.

One childhood instance is still vivid in my mind. To set this story up - it was customary to kick younger kids off the court when older kids, young adults, or older adults came around and wanted to play basketball. In essence, they would just take over the court. One day we were playing on the basketball court at Jones, a local elementary school. A group of guys was picking the two teams, they picked up my friend to play. My friend happened to be a boy. They did not want me, a girl, to play with them. But they realized that they were still short one player. Reluctantly and I mean reluctantly and due to some persuasion by my friend, they eventually picked me to play in the game. Before the game started the other team was on the court matching up who from their team would guard who on our team. When one of the players on the opposite team realized that he was assigned to guard me he was very upset. He started ranting and raving about who put him on the girl, how he did not want to guard a girl, etc. This tripped me out! It was evident that he saw this matchup as a personal insult. Well, as he was running off at the mouth, venting his disgust about the matchup against me, the more he talked the more fired up I became inside. And I do mean fired up! Instead of talking in response to his foolishness, I preferred to let my actions speak for me. This guy had ticked me off, but no one knew it because I was cool, calm, and collected on the outside. Yet, on the inside, I kept telling myself I was going to get him. It became my personal mission to shut him up.

The game began and it did not take long before I started scoring. It wasn't just one time, but multiple times that my teammates got me the ball and I put it through the hoop. Then I heard the words, "Get that girl!"

I thought, "Naw, Naw, you get me Mr. Smarty Mouth. This is your butt whooping and yours alone." How dare you see me as inferior or insignificant as a basketball player just because I am a girl? Still get fired up thinking about it after all these years. He had nothing coming that game, he had awakened a giant inside me and gotten himself into something that there was no return. Without a doubt, this was one of the epic events in my life that helped shape me as a person and a basketball player. I do not recall what ended up being the final score of the game, but all I know is we won. It was with great pride and honor that I was able to publicly shut this guy up and my team was able to say, "Next!"

LIFE LESSONS:

- Don't publicly cause a scene without being able to back up what you are running off your mouth about
- Show respect for each player without discrimination or assumption
- Don't underestimate your opponent
- Beware of your opponent: if you are talking junk and they are quiet this could mean big trouble for you

Way of Escape

This section of the book is the section that is dreaded to talk about and reveal to the reader. However, it is a critical aspect and worthy to be mentioned; even though, it will cause me to revisit unpleasant childhood memories during the process. It is important to note that I am sharing this information from my perspective and recollection and not on behalf of my siblings.

I am the oldest and only girl of the three children that were birthed by my mother, who had us all by the age of twenty-one years old. We grew up on welfare. Something that I hated because of the negative connotation that was attached to it. Except when it came to receiving the government cheese, I didn't mind that part. It made the best macaroni and cheese and grilled cheese sandwiches. Despite our family's economic status, my brothers and I went to school with clean clothes on our backs, food in our stomachs, and had a mother who was active and visible in the schools that we attended. Trust me, it was known who her children were, and the principals and teachers did not want to get an unexpected visit from her.

There was a part of our upbringing that was not so pleasant and hidden from the masses – domestic abuse. This occurred gradually, there were times of peace, of laughter, and conversations as one unit at the dinner table. But there came a point when there was a shift in the atmosphere or better yet the household went on a roller coaster ride from peaceful waters to a thunderstorm, and vice versa. Many painful instances were witnessed especially during the early years of my basketball development. I grew up in fear; fear of my loved one being hurt. The physical abuse did not happen initially but developed over a process of time. How much time? I don't remember. All I know is when it did start it occurred over many years. Seeing this time and time again changed something in me internally.

Even at a young age, I knew that this was not right. I knew I was amid something devastating that would have a lifetime effect. Needless to say, it took an emotional toll on me. My developmental state of mind was not strong enough to properly process and respond to such a heavy matter. I did not have anyone that I could talk to about it. What went on in the house stayed in the house. Disclosing private matters to outsiders was taboo and strongly discouraged in our family culture. Additionally, such disclosure had the possibility of bringing more harm to my loved ones and myself. It could also cause legal actions to remove my siblings and me from our mom, our home and/or each other. The cost was too high for me to take the chance of disrupting the family unit by letting someone know what was going on in the household. Therefore, to combat the dysfunction that I was living in, school and basketball became my outlets. I excelled in both, honor student in school and up-and-coming basketball star on the court. So, when there was unrest at home or I was dealing with some things that were weighing on my mind, I would walk to the playground nearby at Jones School to play ball. This would help me to relieve stress and enter my safe haven. When I was a child, basketball was something that helped me not to lose my mind, literally. It saved my life. For that, I will be forever grateful to God.

As I progressed as a basketball player from the fifth grade, I saw that I could make something of myself in the sport. One day it clicked, this could be my way out of this crazy house. As a result, I set my sights on getting an athletic scholarship. Then I started on my quest to use basketball as a tool to go to college and make a better life for myself.

LIFE LESSONS:

- People tend to put on masks, things happen behind the scenes you have no clue of
- You can either let the negative things that happen in your life set you back or be the catalyst to move you forward, you make the choice
- Life experiences, good and bad, help to shape you as a person

The Playground

The court at my neighborhood elementary school is where I went through boot camp in the game of basketball. This is where I put in countless hours being on the court and where the development of my toughness started to blossom. I was a skinny kid, average height and found myself getting knocked down a lot during basketball games with the boys on the playground. The interesting thing about this is that during these times I would always get back up and continue to play. There is not one instance that I did not continue to play or started crying because they got too rough with me during the game. Yes, they would knock me down, but they could not keep me down. I rose again and again and again and kept on playing, regardless if the team I was on ended up winning or losing the game in the end. The amazing thing that began to happen was that mental toughness was developing within me. The more I got knocked down on the court, the more determined I was to get back up. Usually, this occurred when I was driving to the basket for a layup or after rebounding the ball from a missed

11

shot. After a process of time, getting knocked down during the game did not even phase me. It was a normal part of the game. Not only did I expect it, but I even learned to welcome it.

My basketball friend, Marcus, met me on the court day after day at the school and taught me how to play the game, help me define my game, and help me stand up to my opponents, especially boys. His invested in me through his time and talent ultimately helped me to become the decorated basketball player that I evolved to. For that, I am very grateful, thankful, and humbled for what he did for me. It was not in vain. Take a bow, my basketball brother and childhood friend.

LIFE LESSONS:

- Take time to pass on to others the skills and talents that you possess so that they can grow
- The success you achieve in life is due to the help from others along the way, no one gets there on their own
- "Thank you", are two of the most powerful words that one can say. Let others know that you appreciate what they have done for you

High School

Transitioning from junior high to high school was not an easy feat. The practices, conditioning, and games were more intense. As a sophomore, I made the varsity basketball team. This accomplishment came along with higher expectations of me as a player. I was one of the youngest players on the team, so I had to prove myself to the coaches and the players that I indeed deserved to have a spot on the team. Some players questioned how and why I made the varsity team and were not happy with this coaching decision.

I was not embraced by all as a teammate from the start. I recognized that but I did not let it bring me down. It bothered me because I felt like I was being treated unfairly, but that was something I was able to overcome. I was not satisfied with just being on the team, I endeavored to be a key player on the team. I did not plan to sit on the bench, I had my eyes set on being a starter. However, that would not come along easily. During preseason practice one of my teammates attempted to cause discord amongst the team. She instigated a disagreement between two of my teammates, who happen to be twin sisters, and myself. It only lasted for a brief period of time. The three of us collectively confronted the trouble-maker teammate and her foolishness ceased. Despite a rocky start in our relationship as teammates, the same twins and I ended up becoming best friends, and still are today over thirty years later.

———— ≈≈≈ ————

Throughout the season, the games I looked forward to the most were the ones against our cross-town rival, Saginaw High. There were always lots of people in the stands and they were loud, cheering for their respective team. Talent-wise Saginaw High's team was stacked; I mean in every position. That team was loaded with athletic players. We had an al-right team on the talent spectrum but was no match against Saginaw High. This is not a put-down; it was the reality. They had a much better team than we did, but we still put forth an effort to beat them. The closest our team came in doing so ended with an 11-point deficit. That was an honorable loss. They beat us by a larger margin in the other games.

There was one game I specifically remember doing well in. Saginaw High had home court, as always there were a lot of people in the stands, and the atmosphere in the gymna-sium was energetic. A lot of the players on our rival's team had been my teammates on a summer team. We had known each other for years and had mutual respect as individuals and basketball players. However, when we had to play against each other we did not let our friendship get in the way of playing hard. Once the game started, it was on! I was clicking on all cylinders that game, shooting jumpers, making free throws, and driving the lane. On one sequence as I made my way to the left corner, a Saginaw High fan yelled out, "there she goes!", right before I drilled a jump shot. This was a fun game for me because I performed well. At the conclusion of the game, my team lost as expected, but I scored twenty points.

The day that I scored 1,000 career points was so sweet because it was done at home against Flint Northern High School. There is a long history of rivalry between Saginaw schools and Flint schools. Now don't get me wrong, Flint has a reputable history of producing some talented athletes especially in basketball. In no way were they an easy foe to overcome, they had game. This was our last home game of the season during my senior year. When Flint Northern's team walked into our gym, they thought they had won the game before the game had even started. You could sense it by their demeanor. They knew they were going to win. It did not help that we had a disappointing record this particular year.

There was something that came out of each of us during that game that had not surfaced any other time in the season. We played our best game ever that season as a team; it was a beautiful thing to witness and be a part of. During the latter half of the game, I fell on the floor after going up for a rebound. One of Northern's players fell directly on the side of my left knee. The game stayed in play and all the players were on the other end of the court with me still laying on the floor on the opposite end because I was physically unable to get up. The referees did not blow the whistle so that I could get assistance. My coach did not call a timeout so that I could be tended to either. Nevertheless, my momma, my biggest and loudest supporter, made her voice known during this situation by saying something to the refs and yelling at my coach. Fortunately, I managed to get to my feet to receive a pass from my teammate who had gotten the rebound on the other end. Before I could get a shot up, the referee blew his whistle because he noticed that I was still hurt. Go figure. Mister referee, you should have blown your whistle way before now.

When the play was stopped, my momma was very vocal in dismay especially towards my coach because she did not come to my aid when I was hurt. Momma wanted to beat her up. She was taking up for me on one hand, but she was also embarrassing me. She did not care though, she was going to say what she wanted to say and everyone else would have to deal with it, even me. Momma Bear was hot! After the air cleared, the play was back in motion. I was able to run up and down the court. The adrenaline was going inside of me, I did not even focus on the injury. I was aware of how many points I needed in the game beforehand to break the 1,000 points ranking. After I scored the required points, there was a pause in play for the announcer to say my name and the milestone that I had accomplished. The fans cheered and my momma was there to witness it for herself. It was a humbling and exciting moment in my life and for my family. Something that no one can ever take away from me. An accomplishment that I will cherish forever.

Honors:

- Varsity Award
- Most Improved Player
- Most Valuable Player
- Saginaw Valley Academic Team
- Basketball Association of Michigan All-Star Team

LIFE LESSONS:

- A mother does not care how old her child is, if something happens to her cub, Momma Bear is going to rise to protect and defend
- My successes were a reward to my mother for all the sacrifices that she made for me to play and succeed in basketball
- Do not allow others to dictate your position in life, they do not know what is inside of you

Unity Park

During my high school years, Unity Park, in the projects was a familiar place to play basketball by the locals. During this time of my basketball years, my homies and I were running on the court mainly with and against the boys and men. My homegirls who were also my high school teammates made regular trips to play with and against the guys on the court. We had some good games at Unity Park; they were competitive, sometimes intense, but always respectful. Up and down the court, running fast breaks, getting rebounds, and running impromptu plays. We had fun! The more and more we came to play at the court, the more comfortable we became to play against our opponents and progress in our individual game and as teammates. As a result, we built a reputation on the court as worthy opponents, not just as girls but as fellow basketball players. We were a force to be reckoned with and players that the guys learned to look forward to playing against, as well as have as teammates. There were many victories, as well as defeats at Unity Park. However, the experience of playing streetball with those groups of guys was invaluable.

LIFE LESSONS:

- It's important to gain experience in a variety of places to become a well-rounded person and a better athlete
- It's better to beat the guys on the court with other female players, it makes the victory so much sweeter
- Push yourself and others to excel, whether it is comfortable or not
- Allow yourself to be taught, as well as become a teacher

The Friendship Games

Have you ever heard of the Friendship Games? This was a multi-sport event between Saginaw, Michigan, United States and Sault Ste. Marie, Ontario, Canada. Each year it would alternate which country would be the host country for the events. The host country would also host families and take in the international athletes during the games for that year. This was my only international basketball experience and one that I am so proud to have participated in for many years.

One thing that I learned early in life, was to get better I had to play against others who were better than me. I would purposely tryout for the team that was the next age level higher. For example, when I was 11 or 12, instead of playing for the 12 and under team, I played on the 14 and under team. If I remember correctly, I was one of the youngest, if not the youngest, and smallest player on the team when I played in the Friendship Games.

There was one incident at a practice that has been forever etched in my memory, as well as in my heart. I got knocked down hard during practice by one of the older players who was mean and tough. She had no mercy on me at all. She did not even help me up after leveling me to the ground with a hard hit. She was my teammate, but that did not matter to her at all. It was as if she had the attitude that if I could not hang, I should not be out there. Not sure why she had such a chip on her shoulder. All I know is she had no compassion for me at all. However, another teammate came to my aid and helped me to my feet. Yes, I was shaken up, but I was not going to quit. It made me more determined to show that I deserved to be on the team. The mean teammate may have tried to get rid of me, but I was not going ANYWHERE! She was going to be stuck with me on the team. I was not going to be run off the team, by her or anyone else. I was there to stay!

Throughout the years I cannot count how many times I have replayed or told others about this incident in my life to encourage them in tough situations. This was indeed a defining moment in my life that is still just as powerful today as it was back then. Don't give up, don't give in, and don't give out. Look intimidation right in the face and go forward to excel.

It was exciting to go to Sault Ste. Marie to play basketball. It was like a mini-Olympics experience. There was an opening and closing ceremony, a medal presentation, and a closing party. It was fun to compete with my basketball friends, teammates, and school rivals. I also really enjoyed playing against international players and learning about a different culture.

LIFE LESSONS:

- Broaden your horizon and learn about another country
- Stretch yourself out of your comfort zone
- To get better, you must play against, and with those who are better

College Days

Eastern Michigan University

After graduating from high school, I continued my educational journey the following Fall at Eastern Michigan University (EMU). I was not recruited for basketball but had a desire to tryout for their team. I am not sure how the coach found out about me, but I was able to tryout for the team without actually having to tryout. I made the team but was not made a part of the team.

From the onset, I felt like an outsider. It was a clear distinction between the recruited and returning players versus the walk-on players. There was an atmosphere that the latter were made to feel like second-class citizens for the most part, at least in my case. However, there were a few players on the team that welcomed me and were genuinely caring and encouraging individuals; yet it was still evident that I was an outsider.

I remember the first day of conditioning, the team had to do long-distance running in the gym. I was not accustomed to long-distance conditioning throughout my basketball experience. Ignorantly, I started out running too fast at the beginning, and by the time I had run only one lap around the court I was exhausted and unable to continue in this segment of the conditioning session. There was nothing left in the tank. The head coach told me to stand out of the way during the rest of this part of the conditioning. What an embarrassment! What in the world was I doing? The rest of the team had paced themselves and completed the running portion of practice, while I had to watch them nearby. This was the only practice that I recall participating in. There was little to no chance that I would even play in a single game for the team. I think making the team was more of a courtesy from the coach, not something to be taken seriously by me.

———— ∞ ————

Before the season began, the coach offered me the team manager position when it became available. I accepted it because the managerial duties were reasonable; for example, videotaping the home games, gathering the team uniforms after the games for washing, and handing out water during practices, to name a few. Plus, the position came with a small scholarship. It seemed like a good idea, unknowingly that the acceptance of the managerial position would be a life-altering moment later on.

Being the team manager had its perks, I got to be a part of the basketball team, developed relationships with some of the players and coaching staff, and get into the basketball games for free. However, something was missing. I was not fulfilling my purpose. Deep down within me, I knew I was not meant to be a team manager, but a player. This became ever so clear to me at one practice. I was sitting on the sidelines while the team was practicing when the head coach asked me to come in so that she could show the players how to run this certain play. I did so and realized what these players were doing I could do also. Afterward, I returned to the sidelines to observe the practice once again. As I was doing so, tears welled up in my eyes. At that point, I knew I had to pursue my dream of playing collegiate basketball. My heart yearned to do so, and the desire was so strong, it could not be denied. I had to make a decision and it was not going to be an easy one; I wanted to pursue playing basketball, but I did not want to return home to do it. I enjoyed college life, even though I was not taken my studies very seriously at the time.

Soon there was another key event that shocked my world. One of the graduate assistants who had befriended me on the team approached me and encouraged me to go to see the Assistant Athletic Director. She was trying to tell me something without actually telling me. Do you know what I mean? She did not share in detail why it was so important for me to talk to this person, just that I needed to do so. Upon her advice, I went to the office of the Assistant Athletic Director and told her the graduate assistant told me to come to see her. I was shocked to find out that because I accepted the team manager position, I became ineligible to ever play basketball at EMU. WHAT? I was so hurt! The head coach never informed me of that. How could she keep that from me? Whether intentionally or accidentally, it soured my feelings towards her. Making matters worse, before the academic school year had ended, she asked me if I was going to try out for the team the following year, knowing that I could not play on the team. I believed she knew; it made no sense that her graduate assistant knew, and she did not. Why try to give me a false sense of hope. This ticked me off. My response was to use it as fuel to pursue my passion for playing collegiate basketball. After the basketball season had ended, my managerial duties ceased as well. I never told the coach that I had spoken to the Assistant Athletic Director, and she informed me that I could never play on the team. I am so grateful for the graduate assistant that looked out for me. All four years of eligibility as a basketball player were protected because I was never on the team roster or played in a collegiate game for the university.

After the basketball season, I played intermural basketball with the guys on campus. One day when I was playing, I noticed the head women's basketball coach looking from the sidelines. I tried to do my thing on the court when I saw her. I felt like I had to prove something to her. Look and weep, you missed out on me as a player. Although my value as a basketball player would not be recognized at EMU, it would shine somewhere else. That was a fact! At first, I was hurt to find out that I would not be able to play basketball at EMU, but it was indeed a blessing in disguise.

LIFE LESSONS:

- Follow your dreams so there will be no regrets
- Do not allow others to stop you from accomplishing what is in your heart
- You must want it bad enough to go after it
- Allow others to fuel your determination to do what they believed you could not do

---

Delta College

After finishing my freshman year at Eastern Michigan University, I decided not to return for my sophomore year. Instead, I enrolled in Delta College to continue my education and to pursue my dream of playing collegiate basketball.

My basketball days at Delta College were some of the most memorable experiences. Not just because I was about to live out my dream of a collegiate basketball player, but because I was going to be playing ball with my two best friends from high school, along with another one of our high school teammates. Once again, we would be on the court together. It was exciting and a source of encouragement as well. There is a sense of peace that comes along with playing with players you are familiar with.

I did not want to come back home, but the opportunity to live out my dream was a much stronger desire than the discomfort of living back home during this period. If I did not take this opportunity, I was certain that I would regret it later in life. This was too much for me to bear even in thought, so it was something that I had to do.

Playing basketball in high school and college are two different things. Not only is it a higher level and demand on your body physically, but mentally as well. In the process, you will find out what you are made of and if you are willing to pay the price to live out your dream. This was the case for me. Conditioning was no joke! The team rarely, if ever, did long-distance running, but sprint drills were another story. It was even worst when you were being timed. At first, the coach would see how long it took us to make it through the drills to gauge where we were at the early stage of conditioning, intermediate stage, and then eventually the latter stage. I recall a time during conditioning when I looked over to one of my teammates and I said, "I have to laugh to keep from crying."

It's funny now but trust me it was not funny then. I was pushed to a limit like I never had been pushed before as a basketball player. I learned two valuable lessons from this situation that is still etched in my memory. First, no matter what else the coach throws at me at any other practice, I knew I could make it through it because I made it through this one. Second, I saw that I was made of toughness and determination. These are two characteristics that are still predominant in my life today. I was serious about living out my dream as a collegiate player and no conditioning practice was going to cause me to quit.

My first basketball season at Delta College was full of such great memories. Not only was I back on the court playing with three of my high school teammates, but it was such a joy to play ball with a group of young ladies that had the same mindset – a heart to win. The tallest player on that year's team was less than 6'0. Nevertheless, we were scrappy, and this played in our favor more than not. Don't get me wrong, we had our issues and disagreements as a team. However, we addressed them behind closed doors; when it was game time, we displayed a united front. It was a conscious act that each player willingly took a role in carrying out. This is one of the things that I respected about our team the most. We were all heart-minded to just play ball.

Two teams from our conference that I was excited to play were Mott Community College in Flint, Michigan, and Highland Park Community College in Detroit, Michigan. My teammates from high school and I thrived in such games while some of our other teammates would tend to become intimidated and not play their best game. Nevertheless, we gladly welcomed the challenge without backing down. These conference rivalries turned into some of the most memorable games as a player at Delta College.

One of my all-time favorite road trip tournaments was to Vincennes University in Vincennes, Indiana. We were invited to play in its tournament and the team was very excited to participate and travel somewhere we had not been before. Once we arrived at the gym, it looked like a baby University of Michigan. You could tell the university had money. We were from a community college in a small town in Michigan. Delta College was not even listed on the map. We were an unknown team to the elite basketball circuit. On the first day of the tournament, we were scheduled to play the first game against Vincennes University, the host school. Talent-wise Vincennes was a better team than we were. There was one player on their team that stood out. She had game yet, she had a humble demeanor. I admired her. Vincennes had control practically the entire game. Not only were they a more talented team but more experienced as well. With less than four minutes left in the game and an eleven-point lead, the coach for Vincennes started going down her bench and subbing in her players against us as if she had written us off and already claimed the win. This rubbed our coach the wrong way, he was upset. I had never seen him so mad. He said something along the lines of, "if she thinks she can just go down her bench on us she got another thing coming!"

The team fed off our coach's anger. When we went back on the court after the timeout something ignited on the inside of each of us. It was on! With only approximately three minutes and eighteen seconds left on the clock, it was as each of our players personally elevated their game. We dived for loose balls, we caused jump balls, we made key baskets, and our defense collectively went into another gear. We were feisty. There was indeed a shift in momentum. When the game buzzer sounded, little known Delta defeated the powerhouse Vincennes by four points. That's right, we went from being eleven points behind to a four-point win. We did it! It felt like we had won the championship. We were jumping up and down, so excited that we accomplished what seemed to be impossible.

While we were celebrating and in sheer bliss on our end, Vincennes was in pure shock on the other end. They could not believe that we had come back to beat them. Now, the tables had turned, and their coach was upset. She was so upset she would not give our coach a copy of the game tape, which was customary for the host coach to do after the game. Bad sportsmanship. I bet she wished she had never gone down her bench subbing in her players on us towards the end of the game.

— ∞∞ —

During my second season (90-91) with Delta College, two unexpected, scary experiences occurred. First, coming home from a road trip the team was in an automobile accident. It was a rainy evening and a driver slide into our lane and caused us to go off the road. Our driver was our head coach, who was cool, calm, and collected while it was chaos in the van. He was able to maneuver the van, to keep us from a major accident. My teammates and I were screaming and there was all kind of commotion. I remember I was sitting in the front row of the passenger's seat in the van. As I was witnessing all of this happen, I thought we were surely going to hit a tree. I thank God that was not the case. We hit a pole instead. No one was seriously injured, but two of my teammates and I suffered slight injuries and was taken to the hospital by ambulance.

Having on the neck brace and lying on that hard gurney was so uncomfortable. When my mom found out that we were in an accident, she rushed to check on her baby. She, and one of my teammate's sisters rode to the hospital together. I later found out that my mom scared my teammate's sister because she was driving very fast and ran every stoplight to get to the hospital. When they arrived and saw that we were okay, she finally calmed down. She informed us that my best friend and I were not going to go to the upcoming Vincennes tournament. The most anticipated tournament before conference play begins. My friend declared that my mom could not keep her from going to the tournament. My thought was my momma must be crazy if she thinks that I'm not going to the Vincennes tourney. Of course, I said this in my head and did not let it come out of my mouth. I knew she was being driven by her emotions at the time due to me being in an accident. Afterward, it all boiled over, and she was fine with me going on road trips with the basketball team once again. The one thing that I realized out of this entire situation was that life is fragile. I had just seen my momma at the game earlier, then a few hours later I was in an emergency room. That accident could have been tragic for my teammates, my coach, and me. But by the grace of God, we survived, and I can talk about it today. I am so grateful.

———⊗⊗⊗———

The second scary and unexpected experience that season was waking up one day and not being able to see. I could not see at all. It was like a film was over both of my eyes. I called for my youngest brother to assist me. He had to lead me down the stairs and help me walk around. Fortunately, we lived across the street from the doctor's office at Janes Street Clinic. I was able to get in to see my doctor that day and was diagnosed with a severe case of burnout. I had pushed myself as a player and a student to the point that my body was exhausted, and the temporary blindness was a product of it. He told me that I needed to rest my body. To add insult to injury, he also told me that I had to stop playing basketball for a few weeks. What? Wait a minute. I was heartbroken about the news. This was not an easy pill to swallow. I loved basketball. I wanted to play, not take a break. Nevertheless, I had to do what I had to because my health was more important than me continuing to play basketball.

My fear was if I did not heed my doctor's instructions, I would end up in the hospital or even die. It was not worth the risk. Therefore, I informed my coach and my teammates of what occurred and that I had to take a break from basketball. This was not received well by any of them. This was my life we were talking about, no one else's, so I had to do what was in my best interest in the long run. There were some backlash and disappointment expressed towards me by others, but I held my ground. As difficult as it was, I sat out to give my body the chance to rebound from the exhaustion. I understand better now that this was a total shock to the team, being that I was the leading scorer and one of the inspirational leaders. Everyone had to adjust to my absence, which was easier said than done. There was also concern that if I stopped playing during this time in the season that it would hinder me from getting nominated for awards and accolades at the end of the season. I was even used as the scapegoat when we lost games during my brief absence. Some of the reactions and comments that came from the team made me question whether what I could do for the team was more important than my well-being. Winning was very important to me, but not at all costs. I refused to put my life and well-being in jeopardy because others did not understand why I was doing what I was doing. Nonetheless, I did not allow this to sway me from taking care of myself. I was sitting out for the full time to recover, and I was not going to let others influence me to do otherwise.

On a funny note, during my sabbatical, I went to only one road game. I came along to offer moral support and so I could still feel a part of the team. Instead of just sitting on the sideline, our head coach gave me the assignment to take a particular stat during the game. Well, that was short-lived. I got so caught up in the game, cheering my teammates on and giving them instructions on the court, I forgot all about the stats assignment I was given. After this incident, I decided to stay behind and not travel with the team to away games. Plus, it was torture to watch in person when I could not play. The best thing for me to do was to stay at home.

"O Happy Day" when I was able to come back to practice with the team. I was rested, refreshed, and very excited. It was as if I had a new appreciation for the game. There was a new spring in my step. Although I was all hyped up to be back, my teammates did not share the same sentiment and enthusiasm. They had been playing all along and were somewhat tired. Yet, they were glad that I was back with the team. I was still eligible for the awards and accolades that I was told I would not receive if I took time off. I ended the basketball season receiving those very awards, All-Conference, All-State, and All-Regional.

Another highlight of my career was against Oakland Community College. This team was a thorn in the flesh. It was difficult to beat them. They were a good athletic team but had a cocky edge. We achieved national ranking as a team after beating Vincennes University. Shortly after, Oakland beat us, and we lost our ranking. We never regained it. Of all the teams we played, losing our ranking to them was the worse. It was just another thing for them to flaunt in our faces. They were the only team in our conference that we had not beaten, and it bothered us. We had a 0-3 record against them and only one last chance to redeem ourselves.

It was a home game and the last time we would play against Oakland CC. It was my graduating class. I remember so clearly heading to the women's locker room when I saw someone at the vending machine in the hallway. When the individual turned around it was Oakland's head coach and when we made eye contact, he had this smirk on his face as if to say, 'we are about to win once again.' It was something about his look that set me off inside. On the outside I kept my composure in check, however, on the inside I was fired up.

Our team gelled together this game like never before throughout the entire season. We played Oakland CC like we were on a mission. We took command of the court and Oakland CC found themselves playing catch up throughout the entire game. They tried to make a comeback on multiple occasions, but we would put the brakes on them time and time again. The outcome for us would be different this time, you could sense it in the atmosphere. Our team was playing as one and refused to go down in defeat. In the end, we won the game. What a relief it was to get the "W" against Oakland CC.

We did it! We finally did it! To wipe that smirk off the coach's face was priceless. Bet he was not smiling after the game.

—⊗⊗⊗—

In life, there are ups and downs that a person encounters in this journey. It is not good to just talk about the good without interjecting some of the difficult, embarrassing moments as well. In the postseason we earned a spot to play in the conference semifinals out of town. It was a hard-fought and intense game against our opponents. If you were a fan in the stands, you would have been on the edge of your seat. It was a back-and-forth game, no one wanting to concede and give up. It came down to a last-second shot by me that was short. Somewhere in the mix of this sequence either I or one of my teammates was fouled, but the call was not made. We lost by one point. Season over! It was a heartbreaker. Unless you have experienced a similar situation, words cannot fully explain the hurt that was felt from that loss. It would have been better if we had been run off the court and lost by twenty points, than by one point. Typically, I did not cry after a loss, but this one hit me hard. This reality was hard enough, but when we made it back to the hotel one of our conference rivals was staying in the same hotel. They learned that we lost and were out of the tournament. They were cheering and celebrating that we had lost. This was like pouring salt into an open wound. My heart ached so much that I felt sick. I did not want to eat. I kept replaying the game over and over in my head. Things I could have done, or the team could have done better, shots I should have made, and missed free throws that were costly to the team. I cried throughout the night until I fell asleep. The next day we went to a restaurant for breakfast as a team, I started crying again. I took this loss very hard. This was real. This was painful. This was life. Teammates reached out to each other in consolation to help process the loss. It took a while to heal from this event. Nonetheless, I believe there is a permanent scar on my heart from it.

———— ⊗∞⊗ ————

We were in the quarter-finals tournament in the 1990-1991 season, playing at home against a conference team that we had beaten twice during the regular season. The odds were in our favor to win and move on in the tournament. Our opponent had our number that night. They did their homework by studying our tendencies and stopped us right in our tracks. This was the wrong game for our team to have an off night. Not only did they outplay us, but they beat us on our court by more than twenty points. It was so embarrassing to go out like this, not only individually but as a team. That awful night our season ended. I did not want to face negative comments from family and fans. I did not even want to go on campus the next day to go to class after the humiliating loss. Overall, the season was filled with a lot of high points, but the loss of the tournament overshadowed them. This is not the way we wanted our season to end, but it is what it is.

Honors:

- Dr. Daniel Kinsley Memorial Award
- Scholar-Athlete
- All-State Honors
- Vincennes University All-Tournament Team
- Kalamazoo Valley CC Tournament Champions

LIFE LESSONS:

- Don't underestimate the opposing team
- It is not your physical size, but the size of your heart that counts
- Working together as a team can result in accomplishing unlikely feats
- Every day is a gift from God
- Life is fragile so don't take it for granted
- Make it a point to regularly tell your family you love them
- Teamwork makes everyone shines

The University of Alaska-Fairbanks

In 1991, Delta College was hosting the National Junior College Men's Tournament. The women's basketball team was volunteering and working different tasks at the tournament.

The assistant coach from the University of Alaska-Fairbanks (UAF) was present at the tournament, he came to sign a local player from Buena Vista High School (BV) to play for the men's basketball team. Somewhere amid their conversation, the BV player mentioned my name to the UAF coach. One of my Delta teammates mentioned me to him as well. When I arrived at Delta to work my shift at the basketball tournament, I was told that the UAF men's coach wanted to see me. What in the world! As a courtesy, I briefly talked with him and provided some basic information about myself. He said he would give my information to UAF's head women's basketball coach when he returned to UAF. Oh okay! But it didn't matter, I was not going to Alaska.

The following Monday I received a call from UAF's head women's basketball coach, Coach Tremarello. Out of respect once again, I provided basic information about myself. Afterward, the coach said he was going to send me some information in the mail. In my mind I was thinking, send whatever you want to send, but I'm not moving to Alaska. A few days later, I received a package of information in the mail from the coach. Oh well, thanks but no thanks.

The communication between Coach and I continued periodically throughout the next few months. Whenever he said he was going to do something or send something in the mail he did it. That made a positive impression on me. However, I was not swayed to come to UAF at that point. Nevertheless, when Coach invited me to come to visit the college,

I accepted the invitation. It was not so much about visiting the school, it was to get a short vacation. I just completed my exams and finished my studies at Delta College. I needed to getaway, even if it was only for 48 hours due to NCAA regulations for a recruit to visit a college, it was still a free trip. Yes, Alaska here I come!

In preparation for going to Alaska, many questions flooded my mind. What would the weather be like? What should I pack? Would I see black people there? I remember being told that the weather was nice. However, I did not know if Alaska's nice was the same as Michigan's nice. As a result, I decided it would be best for me to pack a variety of clothing items when I made the trip.

When the time came to travel to Alaska my mom and grandma were quite protective. This would be the furthest that I have ever traveled by myself. It was obvious that they had some concern but they both were supportive as well. My mom fried chicken for me to take on the airplane with me to eat later. Momma fried it that morning and it smelled so good. I was so disappointed when I realized I accidentally left it at home. My grandma gave me instructions to keep my money in my bra to keep it close and safe. As you can see, Grandma was old school. I took Grandma's advice.

The flight from Saginaw, Michigan to Fairbanks, Alaska was long. It took between ten and twelve hours with the layovers. As the plane was descending in the air and I was looking out the window over Fairbanks, I experienced some culture shock. To my surprise, there was hardly any snow, and the houses were regular houses. This was a different picture than what I was used to seeing on TV. TV predominantly showed snow, igloos, Eskimos, and the rural aspect of the state. Yes, Alaska is a state that consists of many cities; like Michigan is a state with multiple cities. Wow, it was civilization here. It was hard to believe, yet I saw it for myself with my own two eyes. After that, I had a better appreciation for Alaska.

When I arrived at the airport, Coach was there to pick me up. I had already made up my mind beforehand that I would not let anyone know if I was enjoying myself while on my visit, because I did not want to get tricked into coming back in the fall. I heard of numerous instances over the years that coaches were known to woo a prospect on their school visit, but after the player committed to the school the prospect would find out who the coach really was. I was not going to let that happen to me, so I was very aware throughout my visit. Without fail, I was asked how I was liking my visit and my response was, "I am not saying anything."

As Coach drove me through town to the hotel where I would stay during my visit, lo and behold I saw some black people in the flesh. I remember saying in my mind, "and there goes one and there goes one." This surprised me but was a welcomed surprise. I did a lot of things while I was in Fairbanks within those two days. I got a chance to meet and play basketball with the women's basketball team, talk with the academic advisor in my field of study (social work), attend the graduation ceremony for that year, meet and take pictures with Grandma Tremarello (so cute and sweet), visit the Santa Claus House in North Pole, Alaska, and try pizza with ranch dressing for the first time. Even though I did not let anyone know, I was enjoying myself. I felt peace upon arrival and knew that this was where I was supposed to come to continue my education and basketball career. At the end of my visit, Coach told me that they had a full basketball scholarship for me; to go home and talk it over with my parents, then let him know what I decided. I felt no pressure from him at all to come to UAF. I could tell that he was genuine and that mattered a lot to me. That told me a lot about him, even though I did not know him well. He was the kind of coach that I would want to play for, so my mind was made up to come back to Alaska before I had even stepped on the airplane to return home.

When I made it back home, I talked to my mom and let her know that I was going to play for the University of Alaska-Fairbanks. She did not talk me out of going, she let me make my own decision. However, I could tell she did not want me to go so far away, even though she did not say it. I was able to sense it. Telling my mom was a lot easier than sharing my plans with Grandma. She did not understand why I had to go so far away to school, especially to Alaska. She did not want me to go, point-blank. Yes, it was going to be very hard to be so far away from my family, but I was willing to try something new. I was never one to stay confined to Saginaw or stay under family. I wanted to spread my wings, try new things, go places I never been before, and broaden my horizon. There was nothing or no one to hold me back, so I was going to go for it.

Coach called me a few days after I came home from my visit to see if I had made a decision. When I told him that I was coming to UAF, he was delightfully surprised. He informed me that when he put me on the plane in Fairbanks, he thought that would be the last time he would see me. That day I made a verbal commitment to play for UAF, and afterward, I received a Letter of Intent to sign and return to make it official. This would begin a special relationship between coach and player; one that enriched both of our lives on and off the court.

LIFE LESSONS:

- As the adage says, "Never say never"
- Explore your options
- Broaden your horizon
- Don't be afraid to take risk, you never know where they will lead you

Transformation

Before I set foot on the campus of UAF as a student, Coach Tremarello had gathered some names and churches for me on his own, recognizing that I was a religious person. Religious was a fitting word. You see, I grow up in church from a little girl. I knew about God, and even knew without a doubt in my heart that He would lead me to the college that I was supposed to attend after Delta College, but I did not have a personal relationship with Him. Knowing Him and belonging to Him were two different things.

I attended my first college party within the first month after arriving at UAF. I do not remember if the party was located on or off-campus, but I do recall that it was only a handful of people there and how boring it was. Pitiful is an appropriate description. I had been to high school parties that were a lot better than that one. That may have been the worst party that I had ever attended. While I was at the party, I remember saying and meditating in my mind that I was not going up for prayer when I went to church the following Sunday. It was the weirdest thing. This played over and over in my mind.

45

When Sunday arrived, I attended church at Fairbanks Christian Center. At the end of service, the pastor asked the question, "If Jesus were to come back today would you be able to go back with Him?"

He asked a second time, "If Jesus were to come back today, would you be able to go back with Him?"

I started to get convicted in my heart and tears started welling in my eyes, but I had already pre-decided days ago that I was not going up for prayer at church this Sunday. I heard my voice saying, "I am not going up there" then I heard the devil confirming, "you said you were not going up there."

Then the Pastor said, "I'm going to say it one more time, "If Jesus were to come back today would you be able to go back with Him?"

It was something about the third time the pastor asked that question that moved me. I knew he was talking about me. Immediately, I got out of my seat and walked down the aisle to the front of the church with tears streaming down my face. His wife, who also pastored the church with him, was standing up front as well to welcome me. She said something profound that calmed me when she greeted me. "See sweetheart we are not trying to make you do anything".

Then she opened her Bible and showed me a passage of scriptures on salvation. That day in September 1991, I gladly accepted Jesus as my personal Lord and Savior. As I look back, this set the stage of what was to come of my tenure at the University of Alaska-Fairbanks.

My first year at UAF as a student-athlete was exciting, interesting, challenging, and full of anticipation. The exciting aspects were continuing my education and basketball career. Playing basketball was my gateway to earn my college degree. As much as I loved the game of basketball, getting my degree was the ultimate goal. Before I arrived at UAF, it was already purposed in my heart that I was not leaving without my degree. The basketball scholarship was the tool that was going to help me do just that. Also, I was in new surroundings and had no clue what to expect in my new location. The winter before I arrived, I was told that Fairbanks had accumulated over 140 feet of snow. Oh, My Goodness! I am glad to report that during my tenure at UAF, I did not witness that much snow. Yay!

I arrived at the campus in August for student orientation, days before the beginning of the fall semester. I was one of the two transfer students on the basketball team that year. Unknowingly, my new teammate and I arrived in Fairbanks on the same flight. She was from Eugene, Oregon. Once we found out that we were teammates and gave our initial introduction, we had a bond. We were in the same boat, transfer student-athletes. We decided to do some pre-conditioning long-distance running together in preparation for the upcoming season. This was such a challenge for me. I did not like running long distance, I was used to doing sprint drills for conditioning. Yet, my fellow teammate seemed to have no problem at all running long distances. It seemed natural for her to run. I admired this about her, and it inspired me to get better at running long distance and not to give up while doing so. During our pre-conditioning workouts, she would leave me in the dust sooner rather than later. She would pull off from me and leave me way behind time and time again. This did not discourage me. As long as I could see her in the distance, I was okay. She was an inspiration to me to finish the workout no matter how far I lagged behind. As team-mates, we were in this together, and the goal was to make ourselves better individually so that we could help our team collectively. Thanks, Homie!

—— ∞∞∞ ——

Now on to the earlier practices. There were several re-turning players from the previous year, including the guard positions. This was of great importance to me because that was the position that I played and would be fighting to earn a starting spot. I was not a bench player, and I was not go-ing to start being one now. I am a starter and that's how I planned on keeping it. I traveled 3,000 miles to play, not to sit on the bench. If the starting guards wanted to keep their starting positions, they were going to have to outplay me for it. I was indeed a force to be reckoned with. My competitive spirit was at a very high level during this time, I had some-thing to prove to myself and others. Plus, my family, friends, and loved ones would be waiting to hear how I faired playing at the next level. It was a pressure situation, but one that I was determined to thrive in. I refused to be denied. Don't get me wrong, I was not then or even now a cocky player. That was not my demeanor, but I took playing ball very seriously. My attitude was for you to keep your starting position, you are going to have to beat me for it; athletically, mentally, and physically. When it was all said and done, not only did I earn a starting spot on the team, but my fellow transfer teammate did as well. All I can say is way to represent!

LIFE LESSONS:

- God, the Creator, desires that all be saved and none perish
- Jesus willingly gave His life to save me and you from sin and eternal damnation
- If we allow Him to, God will lovingly draw us to Himself by the Spirit
- Life in Christ is so much better than a life without him
- Challenges are meant to bring the best out of you
- Work on weaknesses to better oneself

To Have New Life in CHRIST:

"That if you confess with your mouth the Lord Jesus and believe in your heart that God raised him from the dead, you will be saved. For with the heart one believes unto righteousness, and with the mouth, confession is made unto salvation" (Romans 10:9-10 NKJV).

Swimming Conditioning

My first year at UAF, conditioning consisted of running, weights, and swimming. There were two members of the team that could not swim, me being one of them. I would gladly put the life jacket on during the swim conditioning, there was no shame in my game. One swim session while the team was in the pool, out of the blue Coach announced in front of everyone that they were going to watch me swim. I said okay, without a fear in the world. The thing about it, I could not swim. Nevertheless, I made my way down to the shallow end of the pool and removed the life jacket. I remember one of my teammates who could swim being nearby, but not too close. Without missing a beat, I started swimming on my own from the shallow towards the opposite end. I could not believe I was doing it; it was a miraculous thing. I went along and when I was in the deep end, I briefly lost my focus and had a moment of fear. I knew that if I put my foot down, there would be nothing to catch me, so I sped up to success-fully make it to the end. I remember Coach and my team-mates being so excited for me and cheering me on. I did it, I actually did it. I swam from the shallow end to the deep end of the pool on my own. But really, you and I know that I did not do that on my own. I believe an angel was undergirding me in that water from beginning to end. There is no way I would have even attempted to do something like that on my own. To make things even better, the other teammate who could not swim made her swimming debut that day as well. It was indeed a day to remember.

LIFE LESSONS:

- Draw strength and encouragement from those who believe in you
- When you are put on the spot, rise to the occasion

Blizzard Practice

It was early morning; the power was out in the dorm, and we had to rely on a flashlight to get around. Several of my teammates stayed in the same dorm as me, but on different floors. All of us managed to get out of the dorm, despite the lighting situation. However, when we got outside, I was not mentally prepared for what we encountered. I do not know if it was considered a blizzard or a bad snowstorm, but I questioned why in the world we were in it, heading to basketball practice. Practice was either 5:45 or 6:30 a.m. It was a serious struggle to press our way against the blowing snow in our faces, snow that caused our eyelashes to freeze. We clonked our way through, under cold conditions, tapping into the extra energy and endurance that were required to make it to our destination, in this case the gym, also known as the Patty Center. I had never been through anything like that before.

I remember as we were walking to the gym passing by other dorms, there were no flashlights, no movement, and I imagined the students still sleeping in their beds. I wished I was doing the same. Then I thought about the people who thought being a student-athlete was all glitz and glamour. They were jealous of those who had scholarships, those who got to travel all around the country playing their respective sport and got new tennis shoes. Those were the people still snoozing, while my teammates and I were pressing through wintry conditions to play our sport. I refused to apologize or explain why I got a scholarship. The scholarship I received was not free. I earned it busting my butt on and off the court. I did not let anyone make me feel bad because I was given a scholarship. I earned it, I worked hard, and I enjoyed the benefits from it, whether others liked it or not. That was their problem, not mine. Back to heading to practice, my teammates and I finally made it to the gym and who was there smiling, looking out the door upon our arrival - Coach Tremarello! In my mind, I was still pondering why are we practicing today under the weather conditions. He greeted us with enthusiasm. I did not share the same sentiment, I was tired; getting there was a workout. I did not feel like it or want to practice that day. I have no recollection of the practice itself other than we all made it through in one piece.

LIFE LESSONS:

- Walk in your blessing unapologetically
- Doing the thing you love will require more sacrifice than expected

Preseason Game

There was a team from Pennsylvania that I personally wanted our team to beat. It was very personal, due to a past negative encounter I had with their head coach. When I saw the name of the school on our basketball schedule, it stood out to me. On game day, I wondered if it was the same university that I was thinking of, and if so, did they have the same coach that I remembered. My questions were answered after the game had started and I heard, "Get her! Get her!" from the opponent's bench. That was him! After this was confirmed, I let my teammates know that we had to beat them. Not that we did not want to beat any team that we went up against, but for me, this one had a special meaning. You see, this is one of the schools that was trying to recruit me to come play basketball for them after graduating from Delta College. The interesting thing was at first the coach did not have a scholarship for me, but after he found out that I was going to visit UAF, a scholarship somehow came from somewhere. Go Figure! When I returned home from my visit to Alaska, an airline ticket to go visit the university was waiting for me. I took the trip and knew within the first hour of my arrival and interaction with the coach that this was not the place for me. I wished I could have gotten back on the plane and returned home. It was a good thing my stay was only for forty-eight hours. I stayed in the dorm all by myself, with no contact or interactions with any of the basketball players. While I was there, I did not get a good feeling about the coach. The thing that ultimately gave legitimacy to my uneasy feelings was while the coach and I was in his office he talked negatively about each one of his players. I was in disbelief that he was saying such things about his team to me, a total stranger. This was not a good recruiting strategy. I felt that if he would talk to me, a recruit, about his team, he would eventually talk about me to someone else. To make matters worse, after he talked about each of his players, he talked about two of my former teammates, one of which was my best friend. Now, he had completely lost his mind. If he wanted to talk about his players was one thing, but when he talked about my teammates it became very personal. I made a mental note and stored it in my memory bank with a big asterisk next to it. The end of that trip did not come fast enough. When I got on the plane to return home, I could not have been happier.

It was payback time when I realized it was the same coach. I did not want to get the coach for just talking about my teammates, but for talking about all his players also. We defeated this team in back-to-back games, sending them back home with two losses on their record. High five!

LIFE LESSONS:

- Some things are best unsaid
- If a person is talking negatively about others to you eventually the person will do the same about you.
- Negative vibes about a person are warnings, it is wise not to dismiss them

NCAA Woman of the Year

One day I was called to come to Coach Tremarello's office, however, I was not given a reason why. I made my way to his office and he informed me that I had been selected as the NCAA Woman of the Year for the University of Alaska-Fairbanks. I was totally surprised because I was unaware of this honor, and I was selected out of all the student-athletes that attended the college. My coach was so happy for me and surprised as well. Then he shared that the next step was that the NCAA selection group was going to vote to determine the NCAA Woman of the Year for each state. Some time had passed then I was contacted again by Coach Tremarello to inform me that I had been chosen as the Woman of the Year for the State of Alaska. Coach was beaming with joy like a proud father. I was happy with the college recognition, but when I received the honor for the State of Alaska, I was ecstatic. I am not even from Alaska. I know that there were smarter and more talented student-athletes than myself, but I was the one that outshined them all. It was the favor of God. I told you that receiving salvation was setting me up for great things to come while at UAF. In addition to state recognition, other benefits came along with it. First, the NCAA donated $5,000 to each school in the name of the state recipient. Second, each state winner received an all-expense-paid trip to the formal ceremony for the Woman of the Year in Washington, D.C. I would be accompanied by the Assistant Athletic Director on the trip. The overall winner would be revealed at the ceremony. Wow, it kept getting better and better.

I told my momma when I received the Woman of the Year school honor, and she was happy for me. But when I told her that I had been selected as the recipient for the award for the state of Alaska, her excitement went to another level. She contacted the Saginaw News and a reporter contacted me for a phone interview while I was still in school in Alaska. Even though I was not excited about doing the interview due to some unpleasant experiences in the past with reporters, I made an exception in this case for my momma. The day came for the phone interview to take place. I was nervous and on guard before and during the process. Surprisingly, the interview turned out better than expected, which was a big relief. The real test would be when the article came out to see if what was written was what I said and in the context of how I said it. When I came home for Christmas break, a photoshoot was arranged for me in Delta College gymnasium to be included with the upcoming article. This was fun and exciting, I felt like a star. I never experienced anything like this before and I was embracing and enjoying the moment with a grateful heart.

When the article was featured in the newspaper, I was happy with the result. No regrets for giving the interview. I sent a thank letter to the reporter for a job well done. My momma, the one who set all this up, was so proud of me and so proud that her child was the sports section cover story in the newspaper. Not only did she send me a copy of the newspaper article, but I later learned that she had gone around town buying up the newspapers to give to other family members and loved ones.

———∞———

Before leaving to attend the formal ceremony one of my former junior high school assistant principals informed my mom that she had a relative who lived in Washington, DC. She contacted him and he was free during the time my mom and I would be in town. He was kind enough to be our tour guide around the city and driver while we were there. This was extremely helpful to Momma and me, especially being in a big city. Plus, this was my first time visiting the nation's capital. I had the opportunity to see and visit things that I had only watched on television, read in books, or heard others talk about. Things such as black squirrels and the Lincoln Memorial.

Upon checking into the hotel in Washington, DC, I was pleasantly surprised by the welcome package that was received, Champion duffel bag, Woman of the Year t-shirt by Champion, and a coupon for a sports bra. I was later disappointed that I accidentally left the coupon behind in the hotel room. When it was time to get ready for the formal ceremony, I was excited and nervous. I was glad my momma was there with me to share this special moment in my life. When I entered the ballroom for the ceremony I was blown away. It was so beautiful and grand. We were assigned to a table, my momma, the assistant athletic director, and I sat together. When each course of the meal was brought to the table, I took a picture. This was not proper etiquette, but oh well. There was no shame on my part. I was in awe of being there and in such great company of fellow student-athletes. It was an awesome experience.

Once the program aspect of the ceremony started my nervousness intensified. They would reveal and highlight the accomplishments of the 10 finalists, then from the finalists, the top Woman of the Year recipient would be announced. One by one the finalists were listed on the projector screen. I anxiously awaited to see if I had made the list. All the finalists were announced, and I was not one of them. I did not get upset, but I was impressed and inspired by what they had accomplished. After the program was finished, I made my way to the front to take a picture with the Mistress of Ceremony who was a woman basketball figure. I searched for the National Woman of the Year recipient to personally congratulate her and to take pictures with her on the stage. I choose to celebrate her, not hate on her. I remember her being such a nice young woman who humbly welcomed me to take pictures with her. The entire experience from beginning to end was one to be treasured for a lifetime.

———⚬⚬⚬———

During my stint as a player at UAF, I was blessed to have family and loved ones travel afar to see me play. They attended games when we played in a preseason tournament in Kentucky and when we played back-to-back years in California. What comfort and excitement to see familiar faces in the audience, talk with them and exchange hugs, especially since we were playing out of state and UAF was thousands of miles away. Outside of my teammates, coaches, and staff, they were our supporters. The one that I was the happiest to see on our trip to Kentucky was my mom. This was another proud moment for her, just as much as it was for me. I never thought she would get to see me play in person for UAF because I did not imagine that we would play anywhere close where she or other loved ones could attend. To my surprise, the opportunity presented itself and my mom and loved ones took advantage of it. Their presence at the games is a collection of fond memories etched in my heart.

Honors:

- Most Inspirational Player
- Most Valuable Player
- Scholar-Athlete
- Varsity Award
- Interior Sports Award
- Woman of the Year for University of Alaska-Fairbanks
- Woman of the Year for State of Alaska
- Graduate Scholarship

LIFE LESSONS:

- God's favor on your life will cause others to select you for honors, even when others are more talented and athletic
- When you honor God in your life, He will honor you before men
- Celebrate others and be happy for them
- Celebrate every accomplishment, and enjoy the moment
- How special it is to accomplish more than you ever dreamed and share these accomplishments with family

---

Gus Macker

The Gus Macker 3-on-3 Basketball Tournament is a community attraction that travels to different cities around the nation. Undoubtedly, being a player in this tournament over many years was indeed an unforgettable highlight in my basketball career. Even as I am writing right now, I am having flashbacks of some of the games played in the Macker. The only division that my teammates and I ever played in was the Top Women's Division. This was the division set aside for those who had collegiate, semi-professional, and professional experience. Our attitude was if we win or if we lose, it will be playing in the top division. The competition that we came up against in the Macker was top-notch. Remember, if you want to be better you must play against those who are better. Some opponents were downright good. Their skill level was off the charts. You could not stop them; your only hope was to try to contain them. Other opponents had the basketball fundamentals down to a science. Then, there were those opponents who may have lacked in skill level but would out hustle you if you let them.

When we first started playing in the Macker, it took some time for my teammates and me to get used to playing in the tournament. This was a whole new ball game that we had entered. Only four players were allowed on each team, three on the court at one time plus one substitute on the sideline. It was a half-court game officiated by a referee. In the earlier years of the Macker, we did not fare very well. Sometimes we would get knocked out of the tournament in two games, other times we would last a little longer. Being the competitive players that we were this did not settle well with us, but my teammates and I used it as a teaching moment and motivation to do better next time. No matter what, we would play in multiple Mackers throughout the year. The thing that I had to adjust to the most about playing in the Macker was the beating my body would take participating in the tournament. There was soreness in areas of my body that I did not even know existed, plus playing in the hot sun during peak hours of the day was draining to the body. It was customary to take about two days to recuperate from playing in a Macker tournament. Nevertheless, this did not run me or my teammates away which eventfully paid off. When we got the hang of the Macker and elevated our game against our opponents we became a force to be reckoned with. We started building a winning reputation in the Macker, which resulted in many 1st place trophies, some 2nd place trophies, and several good sportsmanship awards. Not only were we well-known and respected faces on the court, but we would encourage other teams in between games sitting on the sidelines.

Many tournaments could be referenced, but it is one tournament that stands out above all the rest. This Macker tournament was held in our hometown of Saginaw, Michigan. I am unsure of the year, but it went down in history, at least in my eyes. On the first day of the tournament, my teammates and I won the first game but lost the second game. We did not have to resume play in the tournament until the following day. Even though we were still in the tournament, many people had counted us out of having much success. You see, for us to win the championship we had to win all five games in one day. Things did not look good in our favor. Having a 1-1 record put us in a very difficult situation, we could not afford to lose another game. If so, that would put us out of the tournament in front of the home crowd. If you are a competitive player, one thing that will get you going inside is when people count you out. Yes, we had a steep mountain to climb. The best thing we could do was to take one game at a time.

Nothing came easy, we were challenged to show what we were made of by pushing ourselves and each other to rise to the occasion. One game after another we came out the victors. Yet, the ultimate test was against the players and coaching staff of Saginaw Valley State College (SVSC), which was the hometown state college at the time. They had a cocky attitude and seemed to look down on my teammates and me as if we were second-class and no match for them. Most of our team played for a junior college, whereas the majority of their team played basketball at the Division I level. I must give it to them they were a good team and full of talent. They had previously beaten us multiple times which made matters worse. At that point, we were winless against SVSC. However, you can either rise to the occasion or sink in defeat. My teammates and I approached that game with confidence and determination like never before. It was a very tough battle on the court that day, but this time we refused to go down in defeat. We elevated our game above that of our opponent that day, which finally allowed us to record our first victory over them. In the end, my teammates and I were crowned the Champions. Oh, what a relief it was! We went from a record of 1-1 on the first day of the tournament to 5-0 record on the second day of the tournament. What a feat! Seven games played in a single tournament was the most we had ever played in a Macker. In and of itself this was a great accomplishment. Plus, this championship was so sweet because we were able to take down one of our greatest rivals and we proved the naysayers wrong. We gained a championship in our hometown amongst our hometown fans, and we developed a closer bond as a team unit. This was awesome!

Gus Macker Nationals

If you win the championship at a Gus Macker tournament within the year, your team automatically is eligible to compete in the national tournament that year. While we were congregating at one of the tournaments, our long-time sponsor asked if we would like to go to the nationals in Hilton Head Island, South Carolina. He would pick up the tab for our travel and lodging, but we would be responsible for our meals and spending money. Say what - Yes, count me in! I was so excited, but I had to get clearance to miss an annual planning and budget meeting that I helped to facilitate at church. I was shown favor and given the green light to go on the trip. Yay, Thank you, Lord! Thank you, Pastor!

One of the funniest things that happened on the day of our departure happened when we went to pick up one of our teammates. She was known to not be ready whenever we came to pick her up for a tournament. But to our surprise when we turned onto the block of her house she was already waiting outside on the porch with her luggage. We could not believe it. Even though we never left her behind when she was late in the past, it was as if she was saying, "I will not miss this trip." It was so funny. I can still picture it in my mind. We were so proud of our teammate.

En route to South Carolina, we picked up my mom along the way. Yes, we brought along our hometown fan. This made a total of seven passengers, luggage, and lots of snacks for the road. With two automobiles, we were able to comfortably make the long trip to attend the nationals. Even though the trip was long, the time seemed to pass by faster than expected because we had fun being together. Once we finally made it to our destination in the wee hours of the morning, we were blown away with the lodging arrangements. It was in a gated community on a golf course. The condo was huge with ample space and sleeping quarters. Wow! Upon arrival, we could not stay up long and admire the lodging space because we had to play games hours later. If we wanted to compete effectively, we had to get some rest.

Gameday arrived and excitement and nervousness were on the scene. This tournament was different from all the others because only those teams who had won a championship were eligible to play. It was anticipated that a high level of competition would be present at this tournament. However, we were greatly disappointed that not as many teams participated in the nationals as we expected. The main reason was that the original date of the tournament had to be rescheduled, I believe it was due to adverse weather. Nevertheless, it was still the nationals, and we were glad to be there. The atmosphere at this tournament was different from the others that we played in, and you could sense it. Excitement was in the air.

Our competition was noteworthy. We had to battle for two days before we walked away with the National Championship. Normally, when we won the championship at a tournament, we would be awarded the first-place trophy along with the sportsmanship medal. However, at the nationals, they load you up with things. We received the first-place trophy, the sportsmanship trophy, the national champion-ship medal, basketball, and sports bag. I was impressed. Plus, we got a chance to meet, compete, and fellowship with our competition. When it was all said and done, we were all a part of the same family, a basketball family.

Gus Macker Finale

Have you ever had a time in your life when you knew it was time to hang something up? Over the years, the team had played in many Gus Macker tournaments. Sometimes, it was not the same combination of players, but there was always at least one or two of the core players present on the teams. Before playing in this tournament in West Bloomfield, Mich-igan I knew this would be my last tournament. My body had enough of the grit, grind, and energy required to be success-ful at the highest level in this tournament. I felt it so strongly but kept it to myself until after the tournament had ended. Knowing this would be it, I had an extra incentive to do well, more so than usual. In the end, our team won another cham-pionship. We were crowned champions once again. This was extremely special to me especially because I played my heart out this tournament, leaving everything I had on the court. I was so sore that after the tournament it was painful to even walk. There were muscles in my body that were pulled and stretched that I had no idea existed. A turtle could have beaten me in a race, for real. I was in a lot of discomfort but going out on top made it all worth it. That is the way I wanted to close out my career competing in the Gus Macker, on top, and that is what came to pass.

LIFE LESSONS:

- Don't give up, don't give in, and don't give out, one day you will defeat your giant
- It is okay to be competitive, but be respectful and courteous as well
- Listen to your body, it will tell you when it is time to call it quits
- Cherish time with family and loved ones who have invested in you and enriched your life
- Winning is not everything, but winning is fun

The YMCA of Saginaw

I was at a time in my life that I had not played basketball in many months, it had maybe even been a year. My body had been yearning to get back on the court, but I kept putting it off, making excuses time and time again. It started with a conversation with a dear friend of mine. She and her husband had seen a movie at the theater and one of the main characters reminded her of me. Of course, I had to go see the movie. I went to see the movie, "Love and Basketball," and instantly that fire was lit under me to get back playing the game that I loved. As I was in the movie theater, I got so excited because different scenes did remind me of myself and of similar experiences that I encountered.

One of my favorite scenes was when the main character was playing basketball in her neighbor's driveway with a male neighbor and two of his friends. The neighbor had a preconceived notion about a girl being able to play basketball, but reluctantly let her play so that it could be a 2-on-2 game. He soon found out that she could play, then eventually took it upon himself to guard her because the score was too close for comfort for him. With the game on the line as well as his ego, he was not about to let a girl win the game against him. He fouled her and scarred her face in the process. She did not cry, but he felt bad because he injured a girl.

The other scene of the movie that resonated with me was when the main character clashed with a teammate on her college basketball team. She was a freshman, and her teammate was an upperclassman. The upperclassman had it out for the freshman. She was intimidated by her potential and tried to make it difficult for her. Instead of taking the youngster under her wings to teach her the ropes at the collegiate level, she chose to try to embarrass her in front of other teammates by disclosing some recruiting information in a distasteful manner. Instead of retaliating against her teammate, this sparked her to work harder in practice. The upperclassman was injured in a game and had to sit out for some time to allow the injury to heal. This opened the opportunity for the freshman to play more minutes by filling in her spot. She blossomed right before your eyes and made the most of the given opportunity. When the upperclassman was cleared to resume play, instead of the freshman going back to sit on the bench, the upperclassman had to sit on the bench and watch from the sidelines. That's right, she took the upperclassman's starting position. It doesn't pay to act ugly!

After the movie was over, I could have gone back in and watched it over again that same day. I liked it that much. I did not watch the movie again that day, but the following week I showed up at the gym at the YMCA to play basketball with the men. I vividly remember as I was waiting on the sideline for the teams to be picked and the game to start, one of the men came over to me to inquire who brought me there. I responded, "I did."

If you made it this far in the book, you know that this ticked me off. How dare he ask me something like that? Mister, you don't know me, but before it is all said and done trust me you will.

When I first started playing basketball with the guys at the local YMCA, it was a challenge. I was rusty from not playing for so long, plus I had to learn the house rules and learn how to play with and against this group of guys. It started out being the same scenario that had played out so many times in my life. I was the outsider, and I was a female. Nevertheless, they let me play ball with them and I continued to come to do so. The more I showed up to play, the more comfortable I became playing ball with this group of males, and vice versa. Eventually, I looked forward to meeting the guys on the court. We had some great games in the early morning. It was competitive play, with little to no arguments, and respect for each other. I was the only female that consistently played with the group. This went on for several years. During that time, we formed a comradery. I could tell the difference from when I first started playing ball with the fellas by the mutual respect that was shown towards me.

Occasionally guest players would show up at the gym to play with us. One day I drove to the basketball hoop and the visiting player fouled me and I fell to the floor from the impact. Suddenly, I heard one of the regular guys tell the visiting player "You don't hit her like that."

By the facial expressions of other players, they agreed as well. It did not faze me at all, I just got off the floor like I usually did. But that day I realized that something powerful had taken place. First, I had fully been accepted into the group as a fellow basketball player, not as a female basketball player. I had broken the male code as I referred to it. Second, the players took upon the role of a big brother when they thought someone was being too rough with me on the court. This was something that did not just happen, it developed over time. Later, the group allowed me to bring everyone together in a circle and lead prayer before we began to play ball. Praise God!

LIFE LESSONS:

- Sometimes all it takes is someone or something to rekindle the fire within to inspire you to resume doing the thing that you love to do
- When someone tries to devalue you, rise above it, and shine
- Don't let anyone limit you by putting you in their box of limitations
- Don't intentionally try to embarrass someone, what you dish out will eventually come back to bite you

In conclusion, I have shared some of my personal experiences of life through my love of the game of basketball. I pray that something in this book has inspired you to take a leap of faith, to encourage you to make your dreams a reality through determination and courage, and to be bold when faced with opposition and ridicule. Do not allow others to determine how high and far you can go in life. Do what others say is impossible for you to do, press your way to greater heights, and a better life through hard work, education, and most importantly through the help of the Only True and Living God. Let what I have done and accomplished be the catalyst for you to do bigger and go further in life than you could have ever imagined. Make your mark in this world as only you can. Rise up and soar. Go for it!

Acknowledgments

My God who birthed this book into my heart and would not allow me to let it stay dormant; to Jesus who paid the ultimate price to rescue me from sin and to live a better life in Him; to the Holy Spirit who brought all things back to my remembrance so that I could pen this memoir.

My husband, Oliver, for your love, support, and encouragement to get this book written and published, I love you Sweetheart.

In loving memory of my parents, Mary Loyd Deal and Carl C. Frazier who brought me into this world.

To all my coaches throughout my life who helped to mold me into the decorated player that I became, especially my first basketball coaches, Lois Faniel and Emma Atwater at Jones School for your bravery to do something that you never done before and for lovingly helping to shape my life as a basketball player and person. For being a significant part of my basketball history.

In loving memory of Richard Mack who coached me for the Friendship Games and instilled in me principles of the game and entrusting that I could hang in there with the big girls.

In loving memory of Joseph Tremarello who recruited me and welcomed me with open arms to Fairbanks, Alaska, helped me to further develop as a player and person, and the special relationship we shared together as coach and player.

Jeff Knox for coaching and helping me to excel at the game through encouragement and challenging assignments, offensively and defensively and for being the long-time Gus Macker team sponsor.

Marcus Terry, my elementary friend who spent countless hours on the basketball court at Jones School teaching me how to play the game and sharpen my skills and helping me not to back down from the boys or be intimidated by them.

My brother, Kijoi, who bragged that I could beat the boys in the neighborhood. He even brought a boy to the house to play against me.

My brother Jamarr, who looked up to me as a basketball player and aspired to beat me one day.

My family and friends who encouraged and supported me throughout my basketball journey, you have no idea how much that meant to me.

All my teammates that I ever played the game with and the bond and lasting friendships that have been established over the decades, I would not have reached the level of success without you supporting me, challenging me, pushing me, and trusting me; especially Velma Burt, Linda Robinson, Lowana (Truck) Ruth, Annett (Big Job) Babers.

Coleen (Co Co) Lochabay for your Tina Turner "Simply the Best" renditions after team wins on road trips that are fondly etched in my memory.

My godchildren, Briona and Darrion Robinson who carried on the basketball legacy through high school, and Davin Sherer, who loves the game of basketball at a young age and who is inspired by my basketball trophies.

All my basketball brothers and sisters that I gained at the original Unity Park in Saginaw, Trinity Lutheran Center, the Neighborhood House, the YMCA of Saginaw, and playing in various basketball leagues; the times spent together on the court as a team and the competitive battles as rivals that took place were greatly appreciated and fondly remembered.

Mike Gillis of MLive, for the research, verification, and all your diligent assistance in helping me to get the permission to use the photos, headline titles, and articles in this book.

Tom Trombley of the Castle Museum of Saginaw County History, for all your research and diligence in finding and verifying photos, headline titles, and/or articles that are included in this book.

All the fans that attended any game whether near or far and have cheered me on at any point in my basketball career, know that your support was and still is greatly appreciated.

Pastors Roosevelt and Henrine Gray, Minister Rhonda Hinds, and Minister Rodrick Gray of Fairbanks Christian Center for welcoming me into your family, bringing me into the saving knowledge of Jesus Christ and the baptism with the Holy Spirit in such a caring and loving way.

All those who planted and watered the Word of God in my life in word and deed before I accepted Jesus Christ into my life, it was not in vain.

Eric Henderson and my teammate, Shelly Ayre who mentioned my name to the assistant men's basketball coach from University of Alaska-Fairbanks, which was instrumental in me being recruited for the University of Alaska-Fairbanks women's basketball team.

To my pastor and first lady, Bishop Ronald and Dr. Georgette Frierson of New Covenant Christian Center for teaching and encouraging me to be all that God has called me to be and to live my life in such a way that it benefits someone outside of myself.

To each and every one of you, Thank you, Thank you, and Thank you!

With heartfelt gratitude,

Awards

Michigan Community College Athletic Association
EASTERN CONFERENCE
Awards This
ALL CONFERENCE
Certificate To

Cherina Loyd

For Excellence In

Women's Basketball

_____
Date

_____
Conference Director

Awards

85

BASKETBALL CENTENNIAL
OFFICIAL CERTIFICATE OF PARTICIPATION

This certificate is in recognition of your participation during the historic 100th anniversary of basketball celebrated during the 1991-92 season.

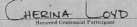

Cherina Loyd

Honored Centennial Participant

Limited Edition Certificate No. 110420

Certificate provided by Phillips Petroleum Company
in cooperation with the American Basketball Council ABC

Cherina Loyd, 22, former Arthur Hill High School and Delta College cage star, took her basketball skills to the frozen north — the University of Alaska-Fairbanks.

News Staff/
Steve Jesamore

MON JUL 13 1992

Cager takes hot streak to Alaska

Cherina Loyd, 23, was named Alaska's Woman of the Year by the National Collegiate Athletic Association.

Former Hill basketball star contends for NCAA honor

Life in the land of "Northern Exposure" is good for Cherina Loyd.

The former Arthur Hill basketball standout wound up at the University of Alaska-Fairbanks by way of Delta College.

And while the 23-year-old hasn't run into the type of oddball characters who populate the hit CBS-TV Monday night show, Loyd has run her way into the hearts of the folks in Alaska.

Loyd recently was named the 1993 National Collegiate Athletic Association Woman of the Year for Alaska.

The honor caught Loyd completely by surprise.

"I left in May to come home (to Saginaw), and I didn't even know I'd been nominated," Loyd said over the phone from her school dormitory room.

"I heard in July I was nominated to represent the school. It wasn't until early in September I was told I'd won for the state.

"The sports information person from the school called me at home, and I was jumping up and down and hollering and screaming.

"I couldn't believe it."

The state award puts Loyd in line to win national NCAA Woman of the Year honors, scheduled to come out in November.

A panel of national media representatives and sports personalities will select 10 finalists from the 50 state winners.

The women receive invitations to Washington, D.C., where the NCAA Woman of the Year will be announced.

"I'm trying not to be anxious (about being selected a finalist)," Loyd said. "I don't want to be disappointed. If it happens I want it to take me by storm."

Loyd's athletic eligibility is used up, but she's still at Alaska-Fairbanks putting the finishing touches on a degree in social work. She has a 3.1 grade-point average and expects to graduate in May.

As a player, Loyd averaged 10.8 points a game as a forward for the Nanooks. She pulled down just under six rebounds per outing.

Alaska-Fairbanks' compliance coordinator Sandra Carter and assistant athletic director Karen Jones were responsible

for nominating Loyd and doing the necessary paperwork to enter Loyd in the competition.

"We review all the women athletes in our program to see which one we want to nominate," Jones said. "We determine how much the athlete has contributed in her sport, her academic contributions and her outside community service.

"Cherina stood out easily. We were pleased to nominate a young woman of her caliber."

The award is worth $5,000 from the Champion sporting good company. The school may spend the money any way it sees fit, Jones said.

"The winner last year was a skier/runner, and we sent the track team to Georgia with the money," she added. "I'm not sure we'll do with the money Cherina won."

Mark Constantine
NEWS COLUMNIST

Life in the Great White North is good both on and off the court for Loyd, despite what her friends might think about living in the land of Eskimos.

"I've had no problem with the weather," she said. "It's a dry cold up here. Besides, if I can make it in Michigan (weather), I can make it anywhere.

"Seriously, I do what I have to do, outside and get back in the buildings as quickly as I can. It might be dry, but it's still cold."

This is the first fall in many years Loyd hasn't either played basketball or worked out hard trying to get ready for an upcoming season.

Instead, she's working hard in the classroom to get her degree and move on to graduate school next year.

"There really is no time for basketball right now," Loyd said. "I miss it, sure, but I knew someday it would end.

"I've tried to prepare myself for life after basketball and one of those steps is getting the degree."

That doesn't mean Loyd isn't still putting up jumpers and fighting for rebounds.

While at home this summer, she played in three Gus Macker tournaments and the Flint MECCA and in three leagues. Loyd was a member of a Macker team with former Saginaw High standout Annette Babers, and Loyd said they won their share of games.